# CHRISTIANS
# DESIRING MARRIAGE

*A Little Guide for the Barren Winter,
Blooming Spring, Searing Summer &
Cool Fall Seasons of Relationships*

EVONNE D. JEFFERSON

*Christians Desiring Marriage*
*A Little Guide for the Barren Winter, Blooming Spring, Searing Summer &*
*Cool Fall Seasons of Relationships*
by Evonne D. Jefferson

Printed in the United States of America.

ISBN 9781498430968

Write or contact for orders:
info@christiansdesiringmarriage.com

For speaking engagements and conferences call:
973-866-9962

Visit:
www.csdmarriage.com or www.christiansinglesdesiringmarriage.com.
Like Evonne D Jefferson on Facebook.

www.xulonpress.com

*To God for the inspiration and the strength.*

# *Introduction*

If there is one thing I've learned that never ceases to amaze me, it's that there is no truer statement than that found in Isaiah 55:8 when God says, *For my thoughts are not your thoughts, neither are your ways my ways.* I think God gets a certain level of joy out of transforming the very thorns and thistles of our lives into ministerial tools for His glory.

After having floated in a vast ocean that seemingly had no destination, I was amazed to discover myself finally washed upon the shore ministering to singles about marriage! I had been crying the blues, praying and pleading for my own deliverance from singleness to marriage and all the while God was setting me up to minister to single Christians, male and female alike, who also desire marriage. I've been a part of or interacted with singles ministries in various churches and I can honestly say that I have never been in a setting where singles were encouraged to marry. We were quoted one of two scriptures, Matthew 6:33, *But seek first his kingdom and his righteousness, and all these things will be given to you as well,* or, 1 Corinthians 7:8, *Now to the unmarried and the widows I say: It is good for them to stay unmarried, as I do.* Oh, I almost forgot what might be the number one go-to,

*I would like you to be free from concern. An unmarried man is concerned about the Lord's*

*affairs—how he can please the Lord. But a
married man is concerned about the affairs
of this world—how he can please his wife —
and his interests are divided. An unmarried
woman or virgin is concerned about the Lord's
affairs: Her aim is to be devoted to the Lord
in both body and spirit. But a married woman
is concerned about the affairs of this world—
how she can please her husband. I am saying
this for your own good, not to restrict you, but
that you may live in a right way in undivided
devotion to the Lord ( 1 Corinthians 7:32-35).*

Many single Christians are settling to engage in all types
of romantic relationships today, all except the one that honors
God and that is marriage. As I pondered this, I could sense
purpose being birthed from my pain and ministry from my
misery. What seemed to lack rhyme or reason began to come
together in a cohesive message. Suddenly, things began
looking a little brighter. Although in terms of a relationship there was nothing budding in my own life, my joy was
renewed as I considered how I could bless others who were
struggling with the same issue.

First, I began sharing my thoughts through conversation,
which then transformed into gatherings in my home. From
there, I felt a tug in my spirit that if I wanted to reach more
people I needed to think bigger and bigger meant conferences
outside of my home. As I prepared for my first conference,
bullet points were burgeoning with far more detail than I orig-
inally intended. It was then that I realized that what I sought
to say perhaps needed saying beyond conferences; I turned
to writing to share pre-marriage and even *pre-dating* lessons
with single Christians.

You hold in your hand this small book of insights and
observations I gleaned from Mother Nature's seasons. One

such truth is that no matter where a person lives, seasons have an order. Interestingly, as I conducted research on the sequence of seasons, not everyone agreed on the exact order within the Northern Hemisphere. For all intents and purposes, I decided to go with the consensus of most on the subject – winter comes before spring, spring before summer, summer before fall, and fall before winter. No matter how eager a season may be to arrive, seasons must wait their turn. A new season cannot come to fruition until the current one passes. As each passes the baton to the next, distinguishing between seasons is arduous at times because, among other things, there may be no noticeable difference between the temperatures. Nevertheless, while the temperature plays a vital part in determining the present season, it is the tilting of earth's axis to the corresponding hemisphere as it circles around the sun that causes the next season's arrival with or without the cooperation of the temperature.

Well, relationships have seasons too. While our mind, actions and internal temperatures may not cooperate, that does not negate the season we are experiencing. Just as dressing improperly for a season can cause us discomfort or worse, failure to cooperate within the proper season of romance (or the lack thereof), can as well. If we become anxious, frustrated, impatient, or hurried in an attempt to bypass seasons, we stand to miss blessings, experience heartache and suffer unnecessarily. To avoid these it is essential that we recognize the season we are in and accept the lessons each season seeks to teach us.

Perhaps not everything will apply to you and, surely, there will be some things you find yourself wrestling to embrace. I do believe however, since every season happens to us all, somewhere along the journey there is something for us to receive. Embrace what you can and pray about what challenges you.

It is my hope that this book will help you begin to see things from God's perspective; that it not only encourage marriage, but will also place you on a path that leads you down the aisle!

## *Getting the Most from This Book*

*Read it through by yourself, praying as you go.* Ask God to give you understanding in the areas you find difficult to do or accept. I know that sometimes our flesh fights against discomfort and some of what I say may make you feel uncomfortable because it's challenging. Wherever you feel challenged, don't disregard the message completely. Pray about it and keep it in your relationship dossier; it may come in handy on a rainy day.

*Share it.* Consider formulating a discussion group of men and women, or use it as a tool in your singles ministry. Consider how our culture might have influenced us in terms of our thinking and conduct in our relationship interactions. Consider whether it reflects a biblical standard. Is there a need and willingness for improvement? Has the church fostered a message that encourages singles to marry or left singles on their own with little to no guidance, and if so, why might that be?

Use your imagination; be as creative as you wish. It will be a great way to meet other singles, glean from their experience and viewpoints, and, hey, you never know what else might happen.

*Lastly, encourage someone else.* Use this book to uplift someone that you know is having relationship problems or struggling with the fact that they are unmarried. You just may find that it will make their season a little brighter.

# *Barren Winter*

L et's face it. The wintertime of relationships can be difficult. Like the season itself, it's a season when what once
was, is no longer. Beautiful leaves and flowers have died; all
that was mild or hot has surrendered to the cold and frigid.
Trees are barren and the ground is hard to the touch. Many of
the birds have migrated south and the varied, cheerful, jubi-
lant sounds of summer have now dissipated to almost utter
silence. There is not much action, if any, going on. Yes, the
winter season can be quite lonely. While one could be dating
in the winter season, this that I speak of is when you have no
romantic love interest in your life.

The *winter season is an obvious and overt season*. It's in
your face. There is no doubt that there is no romantic interest
or prospect in your life. This season can be long, much longer
than a few months, even years. During this time, it's very
easy to complain and feel justified in doing so. You have
prayed, fasted, pleaded, perhaps even begged God and yet,
everyday you wake up to greet the same situation. You have
talked to friends about it, some of whom may have even tried
to introduce you to someone that they thought you might be
compatible with, but all of these efforts proved futile. Your
constant prayer to God seems to render no results and so
you wonder if God hears your prayer or even considers your

desire legitimate. Let me assure you, not only does God hear your prayer, but your desire is also on His radar. He has not forgotten you!

Psalm 55:17 reads, *Evening, morning and noon I cry out in distress, and he **hears** my voice;* Psalm 145:18-19 says, *The Lord is near to all who call on him, to all who call on him in truth. He fulfills the desires of those who fear him; he **hears** their cry and saves them;* Proverbs 15:29 declares, *The Lord is far from the wicked, but he **hears** the prayer of the righteous* (emphasis added). So, you see, God is always attentive to the prayers of His children. Please know that if you are not in a relationship and have not met even a potential person, then please take closer note of the winter and utilize it for what it's worth.

This is what I mean – *winter comes to all of us.* I know it may seem obvious, but during this season, what you do or don't do can make a world of difference. This is the time to draw closer to God. Sometimes when relationship issues or the lack thereof become frustrating and stressful, we may find ourselves pulling away from God rather than drawing closer. I know for me, over time, I became incessantly frustrated with my situation and even felt as if God was being very cruel towards me, as if for some reason my prayer was not worthy of being answered. Though I didn't turn my back on Him, I felt He had on me. Not only had nothing changed that I could see, there was nothing I could do to force God's hand. Yet, after awhile, it occurred to me that perhaps there was a greater purpose I was to serve. Could God have delayed answering my prayer in order to get my attention? Perhaps I was asking the wrong question all the while.

We often raise questions, but not necessarily the right ones because, oftentimes, they are self-focused. So, finally I asked, "Lord, what do You want from me? I have done everything I know to do. I have prayed, fasted, cried, complained, sulked, and even begged and You still haven't answered me. I surrender; just tell me what You want from me."

After inquiring what God wanted of me rather than focusing on what I wanted from Him, God answered. God had a much greater plan, a plan that I'm now fulfilling. Through my pain, purpose was unveiled. Now I get the privilege of ministering to singles searching for answers, who feel abandoned and unheard. I can provide them with some answers and, most importantly, hope. For me this is a great joy.

## Winter Is Preparatory Season

*Winter seasons are times of preparation.* We often think of the spring season as bringing forth life; this is true; and winter is its precursor preparing us for the new life that is forthcoming. Thus, the winter season is a classroom, a time of testing. It's a pass or fail grade but the good news is, if we fail, we get to retake the training until we pass!

Our Christian walk is an ever-learning process, a daily classroom where we must be willing to sit at the feet of Jesus and learn. God wants us to learn things in our winter or wilderness season as singles so that when our spring season arrives we are better prepared. Thus, if you currently are not in a relationship, you have a particularly blessed opportunity to develop who you are, as much as possible, before becoming romantically involved.

Too often, we don't understand that the winter season is an opportunity to conduct a self-analysis, understand who we are, and learn from past mistakes so that we can become the person God wants us to be as singles and as a marriage partner.

The fact that although you may not be in a relationship, you are reading this book which indicates one of the following: you are either curious as to what I have to say or are interested in preparing beforehand for the mate with whom God wants to bless you. You are therefore willing to take advantage of the opportunity to work on "yourself" before venturing into a relationship. Perhaps you are in a relationship desiring to understand it better, or make changes where you may have fallen short, or both.

Whatever your reason, just know that God cares about every aspect of our lives and He wants us to become the best we can be. We must be truthful, however, willing to face the good and the not so good.

*Winter is also a season to bury the dead stuff* and prepare or make room for the newness that spring brings! If you are holding onto baggage from the past and have not taken the time to work it through with God and yourself, chances are you will bring that heavy load into a new relationship. Nobody wants that. I don't have to recount the baggage story, do I? The more baggage we have, the more costly it will be!

*The winter is also a season of maturing.* It may be a little painful for you may discover some things you do not want to know or deal with, but now is the time to work on it while alone rather than when you are with someone. This may be the very reason God has us waiting. When you think about it, that's love! God wants whole people, working and building together. Now, of course, since we are imperfect people, we will never have it all together, but the less baggage we bring on our love journey the fewer the complications and the more time we have to enjoy the trip!

## *Winter Is Analogous to Jesus' Wilderness Period*

*If you can see God using your season of singleness as a time of self-denial and testing, it can be quite beneficial as you prepare for your future marriage.* Analogizing your love life, or the lack thereof, to a wilderness experience may seem like a stretch, but until you find that special someone, particularly as you grow older, the process of getting there may prove arduous.

Whenever God is "up to love" in our lives Satan always tries to get in the mix. Love of any kind is problematic for him because he hates love. God is love; thus, God loves us and Satan cannot stand it. Because God has not yet provided a mate for us, Satan will try to convince us that God does not love us. This tactic is an attempt to play on our emotions in an effort to confuse and make us believe that God is apathetic about our cares and desires, or worse, that God does not want to bless us with a life partner to love and marry and, therefore, will not provide a mate for us.

It could be that God brings the right person in our lives, but we get stuck on minor details we deem unfavorable failing to see the bigger, spiritual picture. The enemy, simultaneously, presents counterfeits in these times. Alternatively, it could be a matter where the enemy presents the wrong person just at a point when you are weak in an attempt to steer us in the wrong direction. However, if we are consistently praying, reading God's Word, and seeking his direction while practicing, ...patience [or perseverance], which produces character; and character hope (Romans 5:4 paraphrased), we will be able to see through the enemy's tactics.

Notice that Jesus was ready when Satan came to tempt Him because He had done his preparatory work. Jesus always communed with the Father; He was a student of the Word. That is why the enemy could not catch Him off guard with matters that appealed to His flesh, ego, or power. No matter how weak Jesus had become physically, He was strong spiritually. Jesus fought the enemy with His spirit-man not His flesh and that is what we must do. Our flesh is a constant reminder of what we are enduring. It can seem as if God is ignoring us. Compounding the situation, Satan mocks us hoping we will stop trusting God, cave in to our flesh, seek instant gratification and commit sin by choosing our own way, ultimately, missing God's best for our lives.

While I understand affordability of an experience provides us the knowledge of how we will act or respond in a particular relationship situation, I believe God provides us with unique and insightful opportunities, particularly, in light of our culture, to get it right from the start.

Satan attacks us based on the video he has on file of us. Oh, he keeps a file on us and relies on our past decisions and behaviors to perform some of his dirty work. He is depending on us operating from a carnal perspective, not having truly changed our conduct and conversation. Because he cannot make or force us to do anything, his hope is that we will eventually succumb to the temptation he places in our midst.

As we know, the older one gets, there is a tendency to resist change. I didn't say we couldn't change, only that we may be more resistant to doing so. Change requiring a Christ-like mindset may prove even more difficult depending on our spiritual maturity. *For the flesh desires what is contrary to the Spirit, and the Spirit what is contrary to the flesh. They are in conflict with each other, so that you are not to do whatever you want* (Galatians 5:17).

As I have already stated, God might be delaying your spouse because He wants you to spend time getting better acquainted with yourself. Since God is always looking out for our best interests, He wants us to bring our best self to the relationship. We all have issues, idiosyncrasies, shortcomings and sins that unless we allow God to work them out, we will bring all of that *deadness* into our marriages. Who wants that!

Because we are all products of the world, many of us, before coming to Christ, had immersed ourselves in its very fast-paced culture, adopted its mindset and participated in its behavior. Conversely, since becoming believers, we now have the mind of Christ, which is antithetical to the world. God's ways are new for us. To attain the mindset transformation Romans 12 speaks about takes committed effort. In fact, it takes a lifetime of effort, but we must be ever vigilant to that end. This means, in terms of dating, that some of our beliefs and past behaviors will face challenges. We can choose to maintain either a carnal or a Christian comportment. This, my friends, is the test.

*The wilderness is a place of knowledge,* likewise, is the winter season. Winter allots us the time to sit at Jesus' feet, to learn His Word and will for our lives. This is a time when God will begin to prune and further develop or mature us.

All of us go through continuous maturation regardless of the spiritual level we may be at for there are always new levels of faith to attain requiring new levels of testing. The winter season affords us an invaluable opportunity to build our character according to God's standard, will and purpose for our lives. It also helps us to have better self-awareness.

Maybe you need to get your finances in better shape, go back to school, or get healthier. So many people put their life on hold because they are waiting until they get married to do certain things. If this is you, I'd like to tell you that life has too much to offer you right now! Aside from the fact that you're not enjoying the present moment, you're pining with the sole focus of marriage, and may be leaving other pertinent things undone that are valuable to your self-esteem and personal growth. The more we work on ourselves the less baggage/issues we walk into marriage carrying.

So often, we pray to be married without considering whether or not it's the best time for us to marry. Take this time that you are without that special someone as a period of preparation to become God's best. If we use our time seeking the will of God, studying and building our relationship with Him while developing our character we will make for a much better marriage partner.

God wants us to continue living life to the fullest even during the wintertime. Be obedient to what He says and shows you as these lessons will ultimately be beneficial to your marriage.

To assist you as you begin or continue your journey, the following chart demonstrates a mature attitude verses a self-centered or immature attitude.

| God's Will | Our Will |
|---|---|
| A surrendered servant relinquishes his or her mindset and conduct to conform to God's will. *Do not conform to the pattern of this world, but be transformed by the renewing of your mind. Then you will be able to test and approve what God's will is–his good, pleasing and perfect will* (Romans 12:2). | Bent on having his or her way, continuously whines, complains, and or prays for God to give them what they want. |
| We have a consistent prayer life and spend time in the Word to develop a deeper relationship with God, discovering who we are in Christ and His expectation of us such that we become the best Christian husband or wife. | Continues living for self; adhering to secular practices, such as cohabiting rather than marrying; lacking commitment to God and others, particularly, the person with whom we are in a romantic relationship. |
| That we recognize that, ...*our struggle is not against flesh and blood, but against the rulers, against the authorities, against the powers of this dark world and against the spiritual forces of evil in the heavenly realms* (Ephesians 6:12). | Fights the enemy carnally, combating with emotions, which might lead to yielding to temptation or giving up hope rather than relying on the power of God and His Word. |

We really can be succeed in the wilderness if we trust God, relying on Him to lead and strengthen us during the process. Remember, Jesus was victorious!

*T*he wilderness is not a place where we get what we want. It's a place where God gets what He wants and we get what we need – empowerment to fulfill His will. I know it's normal to think that the wilderness zaps one of strength, but when we look at Jesus, the wilderness is where we actually receive strength!

God's Word sustains us. Each time Satan attacked Jesus the Word of God sustained Him. Jesus understood that, *...man does not live on bread alone but on every word that comes from the mouth of the Lord* (Deuteronomy 8:3). He understood the value of the wilderness and although He was hungry and fatigued, He would have food again and His strength replenished, but that was not the time.

Natural food sustains us for a limited time, but our spiritual food, which is the Word of God, is eternal, sustaining us throughout life, but we have to maintain a steady diet of it. The Word of God keeps us connected to God, our power source. God's strength keeps us strong and we can declare, *I can do all things through Christ which strengtheneth me* (Philippians 4:13 King James Version). God had not brought Jesus to the wilderness to leave Him! Rather, God led Jesus there to test His faith, His obedience and His allegiance, and through this testing, it confirmed Jesus' purpose.

## *The Garden of Gethsemane – Really?*

*H*e went away a second time and prayed, My Father, if it's not possible for this cup to be taken away unless I drink it, may your will be done (Matthew 26:42). We cannot forget Jesus' prayer in the Garden of Gethsemane. He prayed it during the most critical point in His ministry, the very purpose for which He came. Just before His arrest and His impending death, just before His breakthrough for our deliverance and His return to glory, He sought another way. Though it was on the cusp of what He was waiting for, He knew the process would be agonizing.

It's when we have cried in our deepest anguish seeking the will of the Father, that these moments draw us closer to our breakthrough. The Garden of Gethsemane is where Jesus cried from the depths of His soul to be released from what He was about to endure. He wanted the cup to pass from Him. He did not want to endure the imminent death facing Him. Jesus wanted another way knowing it was the very reason for which He came. Rather than continue asking for what He knew was not God's will, He *surrendered*. More than His will, what He wanted most was the Father's will because pleasing the Father was always Jesus' ultimate aim.

> *During the days of Jesus' life on earth, he offered up prayers and petitions with fervent cries and tears to the one who could save him from death, and he was heard because of his reverent submission. Son, though he was, he learned obedience from what he suffered and, once made perfect, he became the source of eternal salvation for all who obey him and was designated by God to be high priest in the order of Melchizedek* (Hebrews 5:7-10).

If you are complaining, you have to stop. If you are crying, I entreat you to dry your tears and pray instead. Ask God to reveal His will for you concerning marriage and to give you strength to accept His answer, whether it's yes or no. You will need it in either case because even if it is yes, it may not happen right away. Only when you surrender will you find true peace. Do not attempt to have it your way. You will only prolong the process. Remember your goal is to marry, so why stay single any longer than you must.

*Even with all of the dreariness that winter brings it is beneficial.* While I know there are people who love the winter months, I can wholeheartedly say that I am definitely not one of them; yet, I can't escape it. Regardless of your feelings about winter, you cannot escape it either. With that said, learn to appreciate the winter season. Personally, I have found that it's the winter season where I have learned some of the most profound lessons from God.

*Know this. You and your mate will be joined at the side not just due to natural attraction, but also for a far greater spiritual purpose.* The two of you are destined for ministry, for marriage is ministry. By this, I do not mean that God is going to use you in pulpits preaching sermons necessarily. I simply mean that every believer's marriage is a living, breathing sermon, a ministry that speaks of the love and power of God working through you and your spouse. Essentially, it is a witness to the glory of God. Recognizing this during this season is pivotal.

So many people put more into the preparation of the wedding day and devote little time to preparing for what should be the most important relationship in their lives next to God. I cannot express it enough; use the wilderness time to glean every lesson you can to be the best possible spouse.

## *Do God and Do You!*

A s I have mentioned earlier, I have talked to many people, particularly women, who have put their lives on hold in certain areas because they want to accomplish certain things with their spouse. That never made much sense to me. If you want to travel, do it now. If you want to start a business or return to school to earn a higher degree, then do not put off until tomorrow (or until you marry) what you can do today! The very place where you are not going or the thing that you may be putting off doing is where you may find your mate.

Think about that! However, whatever you do, don't do it for that reason; that would be wrong. All I'm trying to tell you is that you simply always want to be progressing for God is a progressive God.

Do not focus so much on the pace at which you are moving, rather recall what I said earlier – **enjoy every moment for each moment has a purpose**. Once that purpose has been fulfilled, every tear we have shed, every pain and hurt endured, every broken relationship experienced or believed for in faith but never materialized, and every moment spent alone, we are now about to see come to an end. The dawning of a new horizon is at the threshold of our lives. We are about to receive God's blessing for He is now ready to reward our faithfulness.

# *Blooming Spring*

I n the spring, trees and flowers begin to display buds, evidencing that spring is on the verge of opening to the beautiful splendor of the season. Temperatures are cooler than summer, so things in the relationship department may be just that – cool; summer has not arrived yet. I view the spring season as one where a relationship is not fully in bloom. It's a time when a man and woman have walked into the same room, made eye contact, smiled or perhaps given a flirtatious wink. Beyond that, nothing more has taken place.

In this season, things take time; every season has an amount of time to complete its cycle. Therefore, we, too, must work within the confines of a relationship's season. That is to say, seasons necessitate boundaries.

Too often, we do not take the time to appreciate the present season we are experiencing, especially if it's a season of waiting like winter or a season where we're making baby steps like spring. We live in a society that frowns upon limitations and constraints within relationships as singles. By that I mean we want to do what we want, when we want, with whom we want, and when we want causing us to rush things before their time. To avoid this, we need to employ wisdom, patience and understanding.

*Not every relationship is meant to happen.* In other words, just because there is mutuality in attraction on one or more levels that does not necessarily mean the relationship should happen. If we try to force it, we run the risk of experiencing unnecessary pain and heartache.

For example, I remember there being a mutual attraction between a man and me. I had a timeframe in mind and was anxious for the next step. I wanted him to ask me out on a date, but wasn't sure exactly where his head was on the matter. So, I said something to find out that I later deemed inappropriate. Philippians 4:6 admonishes us, *Do not be anxious about anything, but in every situation, by prayer and petition, with thanksgiving, present your requests to God.*

Although, he did not seemingly notice my relationship faux pas, it still did not cause him to move the way I wanted and God let me know that what I said was inappropriate and that I said it because I was *anxious.* I was trying to move the relationship forward by my timeframe, which essentially was unaligned with God's timeline. My saving grace was, despite my anxiousness, I never stopped praying for God's direction, nor had I shut the lines of communication down so that I could have my will served instead of God's will. Later, through prayer and observation, God revealed that he was not the man for me. We were at two totally different places in our spiritual walk. Boy was I glad. Pain and heartache were avoided because I listened.

Scripture tells us, *The steps of a good man (or woman) are ordered by the LORD: and he delighteth in his way* (Psalm 37:23, New International Readers Version). It's very hard to take steps when you haven't heard the directives or you chose the route of disobedience. Disobedience of any kind can impair one's hearing. If we are praying for God's guidance, yet fail to hear Him properly, how can we expect to receive that for which we are praying? Also, whatever you do, please do not buddy up to anxiety either. Failing to listen and being anxious have great potential to yield unwanted results.

*Let patience run its course.* Regardless of how long it takes, patience must still be practiced, cooperating within the season God has placed us so that we can receive what He has for us at the *proper* time, *The eyes of all look to you, and you give them their food at the proper time* (Psalm 145:15).

Trust me. I understand that it's hard to put love on hold because love is wonderful, fun, exciting, and refreshing. Love is warm and fuzzy, comforting and fulfilling. Love, when it's good, erases loneliness and lessens pain; it even has a funny way of helping one forget past relationships, particularly, nightmarish ones. Yeah, I hear the amens!

The spring season does not necessarily mean that we are actually engaged in a relationship, but perhaps someone of interest is in our space. In other words, phone numbers may not have been exchanged and dates may not have occurred, but chemistry and communication are there. The two of you are in sight of each other and you know that there's a mutual interest, but just because it's spring this does not necessarily mean that the relationship is ready to develop further during this time.

Although we're speaking of spring, Punxsutawney Phil Sowerby, a groundhog of Pennsylvania that supposedly sees his shadow then renders the dreaded news that six more weeks of winter is in store, comes to mind. Yuck! That is what waiting for love is like – put on hold for an unwanted duration of time, (as if the time you have waited has not been long enough)! Yet, it seems that's the verdict rendered by God for some of us.

Some relationships seem to have all seasons wrapped into one moving swiftly from one season to the next. Two people meet, marry, and despite life's vicissitudes, share their lives together, happily, until death parts them. Yes, it happens; but most relationships don't operate that way. Others take more time to flow into a relationship, fall in love, make the commitment to marry and live the rest of their lives together. Two people may be desirous to take it to the next level, yet for reasons mentioned earlier may find they are not ready. This may result in the relationship slowing down or coming to a complete halt. Trying to rush only complicates matters and ruins a potentially good thing. Waiting does have its benefits. It can show you things you might otherwise not have seen had you not waited.

Suppose one person is more devoted to God, privately and publically than the other. One may want to be in Bible study or pray together when the other wants to be at the movies or some other excursion – most of the time. I've known this to happen to couples. It's difficult for either person to compromise when both are adamant about what they want, unwilling to find the middle ground or see the other's viewpoint. They both love God, they are just at different levels and it can cause a strain on the relationship. Does it mean they are unequally yoked? Not in terms of their salvation, but in terms of their personal spiritual walk, yes, and it can be problematic for both people.

Being unequally yoked can occur on many levels. It does not necessarily mean they will never become a couple, but the relationship requires some necessary, intentional work that *both* have to be willing to do. Each has to agree on what they truly want from the relationship, be prayerful and allow God to do His work within them. It requires patience and prayer. Should either believe God would have them go their separate ways, they should be honest and not string the other person along, the sooner the better so that each can move on to receive the person God truly has for them. No love lost. God's will be done!

Waiting doesn't necessarily mean that the one who has caught our attention is the wrong person. It could just be a matter of timing, which is why we have to wait on God no matter how hard it becomes; believe me, it can be extremely arduous. I'm sure we would prefer being sad and lonely for a few more days, rather than to have to live with someone we regret having married for a lifetime! Why endure unnecessary heartache when we do not have to?

For those whose relationship goes further, I avow that spring can be the most dangerous for couples because of the sheer excitement a new relationship brings. Almost anything new is exciting, especially a relationship so I have a cautionary word to impart.

*Along with patience and timing, we also must be cognizant of our fluttering emotions.* Depending on your experiences, it may be difficult to control your flesh especially when you find someone with whom you really seem to clique. You find yourself daydreaming about the two of you embracing, kissing, and perhaps even being intimate. Eagerness to explore and get to know each other far better than we have license to, as in, marriage license, is always present. In light of the amount of time spent together, emotions may run high and attempt to dictate the pace and level at which the relationship should run. Assumptions run the risk of being made during this time about many aspects of a budding relationship that may or may not be correct.

I remember once when winter was giving way to spring and it was unseasonably warm. Temperatures were abnormal, such that trees started budding and insects you do not normally see in early spring were flying about. The earth heard, saw and felt what seemed to be spring and it responded with a resounding hallelujah! It felt good, and yet it wasn't right. Unfortunately, it threw everything out of whack and the region went haywire. This went on for about a week and then flowers began freezing and insects retreated. Finally, things returned to normal, but not absent of some residual damage. Everything gets out of order and discombobulated when Mother Nature's seasons are off track.

Need I tell you that a relationship can also be off course? It can feel good and still not be right. The emotional, sexual, spiritual, social, and financial states of a relationship are some of the more common areas where couples get out of step with each other.

If we want a serious godly relationship, then we must regard it seriously and that means keeping God front and center. We do not want to end up with the wrong person or even the right person at the wrong time because we allowed our emotions to lead us. Emotions are fickle and often unreliable! We do not want a relationship that is haywire, but one that is flowing, steady and stable.

Remember, wisdom, patience and boundaries need exercising in every season, particularly, in the spring and summer seasons when emotions are high.

Always, I repeat, always pray and ask God not to allow your heart to get ahead of your head. The heart is the place where our emotions lie. We want to be guided by the Spirit of God so that if He says slow down or back off we will without hesitation and no regrets.

Even if God has revealed to you that the person you are seeing is your mate, you still must be careful not to get ahead of God. God is not trying to prevent us from experiencing love and enjoyment. Rather He wants to protect us. Regardless of the stage of a relationship, always pray and listen because prayer is God's vehicle to receive instruction from start to finish. Let's commit to allow God to guide and direct us, for He will if we allow Him. At the proper time, He will give us our heart's desire.

*Be humble.* Recall the situation I mentioned earlier where I wanted the relationship to move according to my plan. It was humility and wanting God's best for me that I was able to hear from God. Had I complained and sulked because the situation was not moving according to my pace and will, I would have missed hearing God clearly, which brings me to another closely related point.

*Be careful not to complain.* Again, you must allow your season to run its course. Complaining clouds the gateway to your spiritual ear. It's difficult for us to hear God when we are complaining. Trust that God is ultimately in control. Trusting Him means fully depending on Him through the *entire* process for, yes, even romance is a process. God is the mover behind the canvas of our lives.

*As a woman, allow men to pursue you!* Brothers, I need your help here. Today, we live in a world where men think that they are the prize and women are largely responsible for this. I do not care how few men we think there are to women, know that if God promised you marriage, then your man is out there and when he finds you, he will pursue you! Granted some men are shy and may not know what to say to you but even if that is the case, somehow he will let you know he is interested. Even in cases where he may not be completely confident in his approach and unsure if the woman he is interested in is attracted to him, a man will take the time to do what he deems necessary to let her know of his interest in her. Now this does not mean that we have to let men do all of the work. He does need to know that his interest is not one-sided because if a man feels his advances are unrequited, at some point his pursuit will cease.

As women, we need to give men something to work with, but unfortunately, many women today leave little to be pursued! Men like a pursuit; it's part of their DNA. This is what I mean about spring being exciting. When chased by the right one it's fun!

I have had many experiences where men have been interested in me, but I not in them. When it was emphatically lucid that I did not feel the same way the pursuit immediately ceased. Sometimes the men developed an attitude to the point that they no longer spoke to me, which I always found puzzling. Their actions only proved that I made the right decision!

Admittedly, some men are rather slow and timid. This could be for a number of reasons. With women being educated, financially stable, owning their homes and cars, the things decades ago marriage used to assist her in acquiring, she has gained on her own. Men are not necessarily the breadwinners in households any longer, so to speak. Many women, having earned college degrees affording them top-level positions among all spectrums of the workforce, earn more money than some men do. Because men get their self-esteem from being a provider, some feel challenged or perhaps even threatened by what he may not have or "things" he is unable to give.

Women, consider how many times you have heard, "She acts like she doesn't need a man." I often wondered what men meant when they would make such statements. They used to irritate me until one day it occurred to me that men want and need to feel needed.

In today's culture, many men, in terms of "things", feel as if they have little or nothing to offer a woman since most of the things she would need no longer requires his money or a combination thereof to obtain. As it pertains to manual tasks, it's just as easy to hire someone to do it or attempt the job herself. In his eyes, if a woman, ostensibly, can buy and do everything for herself, then why is he needed? A man needs to know that the woman in his life believes that he adds significant value to her life and their relationship that she otherwise would not have.

On the other hand, men need to understand that just because more women are in the workforce in prominent, powerful positions than ever before, earning their own money and acquiring things, does not mean they are not needed, quite the contrary. As a woman, I can tell you I need a man in many more significant ways than my career or acquired things can afford me because at the end of the day, I can lose either one of them just as fast as I got them. I would still be without that one significant person in my life, which would make bearing the situation much better.

Given the preference of having material things verses being with her man, I would venture to say, most women want their man! Here are just few reasons: love, which essentially encapsulates everything like companionship, romance, sexual intimacy, physical strength, and intellectual conversation. I need a man to share my dreams and to inspire and encourage me but I also need him so that I can reciprocate the very things that I desire. Some of these attributes we can obtain from family and friends, of course, but not romantic love of a very intimate and spiritual nature. What a blessing it is to pour into someone else's life who you love on an eros level, to grow together, spiritually, emotionally and physically. I *need* a man to share my life, to share me!

Let me be clear. There is a big difference in needing someone and neediness. From the very beginning, God made it clear that it's not good that man be alone and when He said it, He wasn't talking about being without the company of family and friends. God was speaking of a much more intimate nature. God designed men and women to be in intimate relationships and it's a foundational need for humanity.

*Men, give you freely.* Men, there is a woman who needs you and there is a woman you need! So men, stop thinking of a relationship solely from a "things" perspective and begin to think about it from a love perspective, for is that not the foundation of a relationship anyway? What is most important is you! People are in relationships with other people, not inanimate objects.

Remember, love is something that we do; love is a verb and it requires action. Consider Christ's greatest act of love, His death. His dying was active, demonstrated by His submission to God's will, submission to humanity's pride, submission to a cross of shame and humiliation and submission to death.

Truth be told, I cannot deny we women like things, or should I say, we love things. More importantly, however, at the end of the day, a woman wants you and the best you that you can give her is not found in the things you give, but instead by what you do. Sure, the flowers you purchased are something you have done, an act, and she appreciates it. What most women prefer above material things is an attentive, listening ear from the one she loves when she simply wants to talk; she wants a loving man to hold when she desires it or share in a dream or idea she has. That is giving her you. It demonstrates unselfishness because it takes selfless action, devotion of thought and time away from you to give her you. Women just want you. She doesn't want you to ignore her or to brush her off, that's rude. A friend once said to me, "A woman can live with a man in a car," (provided he is a good man). What she means is things are nice, but a woman is willing to forgo things and even endure hard times to be with the man she loves.

*Be present.* We will be surprised at the many opportunities God sets up for us to be in each other's presence. Just being in his or her presence is quite exciting. No words are necessary to exchange, just being in each other's space is enough. It's the knowledge that he is watching you and vice versa or partaking in what is sometimes just trivial conversation that makes it special.

As a woman, have you ever sensed a man of mutual interest wanting to say something to let you know you are in his view and on his mind? It's obvious that he is so enamored with you that he does not quite know what to say, but because he wants to take advantage of the moment, he conjures up something to say even if it's a little silly. It may be something that you have talked about in the past, which is actually a clue that he likes you because he remembered. These are times in the spring when you simply must learn to appreciate even the simplest things.

Although you may want him to ask you out, he instead may simply compliment you in some way. Accept the compliment.

He's expressing his attraction to you. Though you may want more, it is nonetheless exciting because he is evincing that he's thinking about you. I'm sure we all can remember such times when a man's compliment made us smile because he took notice of us and didn't mind showing it! Essentially, these are times we just need to appreciate the moment. That is my counsel to you. If a relationship is meant to develop, it will happen in God's time.

*In any given season, a keen, spiritual ear is essential. It's critical that we listen for God's voice and instructions.* God says, *My sheep recognize my voice. I know them, and they follow me* (John 10:27, The Message Bible). Spring is certainly a time for spiritual alertness and it's a time to be in position; thus, listening skills are imperative.

That said; note all that is happening in your spring season. Do not just observe the buds, but also notice their colors, varied shapes, sizes and dimensions. Every facet of the bud is beautiful as is everything else taking form and shape around them. Familiar sounds are beginning to return like the chirping of birds and the buzzing of insects. Playing children's laughter is refreshing lighting a responsive smile on your face. All these beautiful things should cause us to take the time to praise God for every bit of it.

Though you may still be waiting for the full blossoming of summer, the waiting period becomes more joyful, expectation is heightened and every moment is precious because with each passing day of spring you are brought closer to summer's horizon.

# Searing Summer

*F* *inally, we breathe.* I recall one of the longest, coldest and storm-ridden winters we'd had in a long time. Countless others concurred, it was miserable. To say that we could not wait for spring is an understatement. Even lovers of winter expressed the desire for winter to give way to warmer, sunnier days. Then it came, and what a summer it was.

That year I vacationed the first week of July in Georgia, just a few weeks after the first day of summer and the weather was unbelievable! Sun-kissed skies every day, temperatures well into the 80's. Though some consider that too hot, it was perfect for me! It was simply delightful. I couldn't help but compare it to a new and budding relationship in full bloom, the sweet fragrance of love looming in the atmosphere and the promise of reciprocated feelings from the one you have admired for so long.

Daydreaming or having a vision is fun and sometimes even necessary, but nothing beats the real thing. Sharing and discovering, filling in the blanks of the unknown, and much more are now on the horizon. It's what you and I have been waiting for and the time has finally come. It's a joyous time, but also one that is a little scary too.

The Lover and the Beloved of the Song of Songs come to mind. Let me say from the outset that this book is approached from varied amounts of interpretation as to how one reads and understands the language of the text, be it literal, alle-gorical, typological, etcetera. Admittedly, I am not a scholar; however, I embrace the literal rendering of the text. With that said, I assert these two lovers were real people, a couple by which we can learn much about a romantic relationship as they were in the throes of a budding one filled with love, wonder, promise, and discovery, while also embattled with outside forces and inward struggles.

*Catch for us the foxes, the little foxes that ruin the vine-yards, our vineyards that are in bloom (Song of Songs 2:15).* Outside forces, represented by the "foxes", seek to destroy the vineyard or relationship that the two lovers are trying so hard to cultivate. Metaphorically speaking, the foxes refer-enced in the text can be people or circumstances. Even in the glow of summer, we must be on guard for either one.

*Protect your relationship that is so tenderly blossoming with splendid promise, particularly in the early stages.* Be very vigilant to keep outsiders out of it, especially in terms of advice, unless it's from a professional or someone you respect and trust; someone who not only has your best inter-ests at heart, but who can also remain neutral. As always, the best advice and guidance you can seek is God's and should He desire that you seek the advice of someone else, He will direct you. You may find that you need more advice during the fall season of your relationship than now, but, neverthe-less, keep it handy for eventually you will surely need it.

As mentioned earlier, the foxes represent people or cir-cumstances; yet, we must understand that, ultimately, all negative or evil intent stems from the devil. People are not the devil, but certainly, he can influence people to do his dirty work. Since this is so, I thought it essential that I relay this to you, not so that we focus more on what he does but simply so that we are aware and on guard regarding his tac-tics. Ultimately, we should focus more on what God is doing, for God is at work in us and He is always for us. Too often, we focus more on what the devil is doing when in actuality we need only keep our eyes on God.

*As for the inward struggles, sometimes they are of our own making.* We walk on eggshells, careful about every word we say. Cautiously we watch the things that we do as if, should our love interest discover what we deem unlikable characteristics or idiosyncrasies about us, they might kick us to the curb before getting to know us for all of our wonderful qualities, which far outweigh the bad.

We know we have so much to offer that we do not want our shortcomings to eclipse our assets. Here is my advice, try not to over think things. Oftentimes, what we think someone may or may not be thinking or doing we discover is no more than an overactive imagination. To allay such anxieties, remember that an essential part of a developing relationship involves acceptance of who each other is and being honest with each other and ourselves in the process.

Conversely, if you intuitively sense in your spirit that something is not right about the person or a situation concerning the two of you, you need to take heed and be honest with yourself about it. Honesty is critical. If you cannot be honest with each other then you certainly do not need to proceed any further with the relationship. It's been said many times, relationships should be built on trust and integrity. If these are absent then you really have no relationship.

Candidness can (or should) be the litmus test of your burgeoning romance. Because this season is more serious, you will begin to learn more and more about each other. What you learn may cause you to question whether you want to go further.

Suppose the revelation discloses something that you are not willing to accept, or at least that is what you believe at the moment. Maybe there is prior drug use that has brought unwanted health issues that has the potential of putting your health at risk, or maybe there is financial irresponsibility that will require counseling but your partner does not see it as a problem. This behavior can be destructive causing financial and emotional strain on the relationship in the future, if left unchecked, which you may not wish to subscribe to if your partner fails to seek help. Another case may be that your partner does not frequent church; attendance is sporadic at best. They prefer going to the beach, spending time at the mall or playing golf. Their spiritual relationship with God is not one they deem a high priority outside of believing in His existence.

It's situations like these that we discover that our values are vastly different. Love can blind some of us to things we believe we can handle, when in actuality we find we cannot or we determine we do not want to in the end. In either case, we do not have to feel guilty about either perspective. It pays to know who we are well enough to know what we want. However, what is most important is what God wants. If God deems a discussion necessary, ask Him to lead you as to when and what to say.

*Prayer is essential.* I cannot express enough the importance of prayer! God's guidance is essential so that we don't throw the baby out with the bath water, or translated, let a good man or woman go because of overacting or mishandling a situation that can be resolved. Find out what God is saying because He does have a way of changing hearts and situations according to His will. In fact, it just may be the very thing God wants to use as a maturing or balancing tool for the two of you. This is why it's critical that you remain prayerful throughout every season of your relationship, but especially, during the summertime.

*Relationships require vulnerability.* Perhaps one of the most important things we need to be ever mindful of is that summertime is a season where we become vulnerable; after all, love is inherently vulnerable. What I mean is the wider we open the door to our hearts, the more susceptible we become

to hurt because love requires a certain level of trust and to
trust is to risk being hurt. To love then evinces a level of trust
we give to our partner like no other, such that to love is to be
forgiving, gentle, patient, understanding and kind. In fact, 1
Corinthians 13: 4-8a, says it best:

> *Love is patient, love is kind. It does not envy, it
> does not boast, it's not proud. It does not dis-
> honor others, it's not self-seeking, it's not easily
> angered, it keeps no record of wrongs. Love
> does not delight in evil but rejoices with the
> truth. It always protects, always trusts, always
> hopes, always perseveres. Love never fails.*

Since love is these things, they will need to be practiced when an offense has been committed against us. We
see then that this kind of love, *agape* love, endures much.
It's a maturing love. As we mature in our faith, love should
become more courageous for 1 John 4:18 says, *There is no
fear in love. But perfect love drives out fear, because fear
has to do with punishment. The one who fears is not made
perfect in love.*

We want the comfort of that special someone with whom
we can let our hair down. No one should be with anyone
whereby he or she cannot be true to the person they really
are. With that said, while we want to be spiritually astute,
careful not to accept simply anyone in our lives, we still need
to allow for each other's humanness and not pin one another
down to unreasonable standards. We must remember no one
is perfect, which, by the way, goes for us as well. The same
grace we extend to ourselves, we must be careful to ascribe
to the one we're dating.

*Summer is a time to loosen up and relax more.* The fact
that we are finally in a relationship is fabulous, so let us enjoy
the journey! While we may still be a bit cautious, it's also

a time when we release more of our inhibitions. It is a time, I declare, that summer exists to let in more of the rays and purposely extend the days for lovers.

*Loosen up, but don't get too relaxed!* The lovers in our text are doing just that, but there is a strong warning given three times within the book. The Beloved provides cautionary advice to the daughters of Jerusalem in the Song of Songs, *Daughters of Jerusalem, I charge you by the gazelles and by the does of the field: Do not arouse or awaken love until it so desires* (Song of Songs 2:7 and 3:5; 8:4 omits, *by the gazelles and by the does of the field*). Love here, from a human standpoint, can mean love for another human being, for oneself or for sexual intimacy.

Interestingly, the three times this warning is given, it is by the woman. From the context in which she speaks, her advice, ostensibly, is from a sexual perspective. Could it be because she believes that the unmarried woman holds the key to sexual intimacy in a relationship remaining pure? Now I don't have statistics on this, but most of the women I have spoken to that had sex before marriage said it was the man who was the initiator. I think it's safe to say, in most cases that is probably true even among Christian brothers. Hence, it has always been my conviction that if a woman remains resolute to remain abstinent, chances are better that the couple can end up pleasing God by not fornicating.

*Leave sexual intimacy for the proper time – marriage.* It will be that more meaningful and, most importantly, it will honor God!

Yes, I know it's the 21st century, but what has that to do with the tea in China, as they say? We are God's children, which makes all of the difference in the world! While pondering what makes waiting until married to make love to the one you are willing to commit the rest of your life to worth the wait, the Beloved and her Lover provided the answer for

me. First, we need to go to chapter three where I found something especially interesting.

Recall, the Beloved warns us not to awaken love before
its time. Many scholars assert that in chapter three, the
woman has had a bad dream. Others ascribe the situation as
a description of her mental state. At any rate, the location
of her lover is unknown. As anyone in love, she could not
rest peacefully until she discovered his whereabouts, so she
searched the town square in the middle of the night. While
there, she finds him. Relieved, she joyously latches onto
him, never letting him go until, ...*I had brought him to my
mother's house, to the room of the one who conceived me.
Daughters of Jerusalem, I charge you by the gazelles and by
the does of the field: Do not arouse or awaken love until it so
desires (3: 4b-5)*. She brings him to her mother's bedroom!
What? Really?

Some commentators believe that in chapter two, King
Solomon asked for her hand in marriage, but she does not
accept. Perhaps she concluded, upon self-assessment, that
she was not good enough for him. Whatever the reason, many
believe that in chapter three, upon further consideration, she
changed her mind evidenced by the affection shown him.
Whatever the case, it's what she does afterwards that I find
startling. She takes the king to the place of her conception!

In view of the definition for love given earlier – *sexual
intimacy,* the question begging an answer is why would she
bring him to her mother's bedroom knowing full well that it's
a place lovers physically express their love and sexual desire?
How can one make it any more explicit than, "to the room
of the one who conceived me?" Are they that brazen to flirt
with temptation in such a way, particularly, at a time when
they are so vulnerable? Was she utterly clueless to her own
feelings? Why would she give such a stern warning about
awakening love before "it so desires", yet, place herself in
such a compromising position?

Vulnerability usually pays us a visit during a crisis, a time when we are flustered and our guard is off kilter. She was already frantic because she did not know where her lover was. The elation of finding him, and then, engulfed in his arms, was likely to evoke all types of emotions. Are we to believe she was not feeling some kind of way? I mean we already know what she thought of his physique. Did you read how she describes him? Wow! And we won't even go there in terms of his affections for her. I'm just being real. Remember, they are in the summer of their relationship.

So, what is our friend, the Beloved, trying to convey to us? Why this warning? May I propose that upon the Beloved's reassessment of her feelings for the king, and while enveloped in his arms – his muscular, strong arms – she experienced the arousal of feelings not called upon by volition, now speaking, ever so loudly, to both her body and her mind. Almost overtaken by her emotional state, as if awakened out of a stupor, stunned, she comes to herself and recognizes that going to her mother's bedroom was not a good idea. As the final jolt just before succumbing to what would have been a foolish and regretful mistake she remembers her earlier admonition and, thus, vehemently warns the reader for a second time to wait to awaken love for the proper time. Desirous that her charge be taken seriously, she carefully considers what she can draw upon to illustrate her point most lucidly and effectively.

Although humanity is God's highest creation, He also placed us in a habitat whereby nature is a perpetual classroom for both instruction and learning, a truth of which the Beloved is vastly aware. Accordingly, she chooses the gazelle and doe, two animals that intuitively mate at specific times of the year, called the rut.

Instinctively within the species, particular behaviors occur during the rutting season. The doe understands that mating occurs within a certain time period. Mating does not simply occur because they have genitals or sexual desire; rather they understand that mating has a more meaningful purpose. Even the process of selection is intentional, and timing is everything. For the doe, there is a right season to mate. Just as bears hibernate in the winter, not the spring, summer or fall, does do not mate unless the season is right.

What a lesson the Beloved seeks to teach us. Of course, for humans, sex is not meant solely for procreation. Sex is also God's most creative and ingenious gift for a man and a woman to express their love for one another. For in no greater exemplary manner can two becoming one flesh be deeper, more intimate, more communicative, or more beautiful. Sex is a precious gift that when understood from God's perspective, is not to be taken lightly or for granted. Sex was never meant to be casual, given out to just any person of our choosing simply because we are adults with emotions and can make our own choices. Given the fact that the Beloved had a lover with whom she was deeply in love and that her body was hers to give, she still understood that intimacy had a right time and a right circumstance under which actualization occurred.

Strongly believing sex has a proper time, evident by the triple warning to the daughters of Jerusalem (and as a reminder to herself), the Beloved displays an inward conflict. She desires to express her love for her Lover, sexually, yet struggles with fulfilling the inner urge of her desire and waiting for the proper time to do so for she realizes that there is both a proper and improper time to engage.

*Be careful to whom you listen.* With the plethora of information we receive from the media and society, unfortunately, the time for sex for many is at whim; this has been the rule by which many govern themselves. Simply, "Love the one you are with," as they say. Neither love nor commitment has anything to do with it according to this mindset; it's all about personal gratification. To the contrary, no one who believes that sex is simply between two consenting adults is attuned with Scripture.

Experts say that with as many partners as one has sex, potentially, all subsequent partners become partners as well. In cases where one has contracted a sexually transmitted disease or STD, although it may not have originated with him or her, within a certain timeframe subsequent partners are at risk of contracting it too. The transference of STD's can occur with the joining of one with the other, hence, when the "two become one flesh."

Sexual intimacy has power. We may not think of it that way but consider why some people find it hard to get over a past partner or a one nightstand. Sex has the ability to create an inextricable bond, sometimes referred to as, a soul-tie – a spiritual connection created between two people as a result of having sex. This is not necessarily a bad thing when two people are under the covenant of marriage, but marriage is not a prerequisite for the occurrence of this spiritual-sexual phenomenon.

In chapter six of 1 Corinthians, verses 15-20, Paul, speaking on the subject of sexual immorality, by use of the illustration of prostitution, a practice very familiar to the Corinthians, first, delineates the relationship our bodies have with God. Second, he tackles the subject of sexual immorality or fornication between a believer and unbeliever, and third, through our spiritual connection to God, Paul expounds why, as part of God's body, we are to conduct ourselves in a manner that honors Him.

With profundity and pithiness, Paul illuminates verse 11 as it regards the transformation that occurred since they received salvation through Jesus Christ. Moving swiftly, he then transitions from their spiritual relationship to their natural relationship as it relates to their bodies and Christ, but not as if the two are somehow disconnected, rather to show just how intimately connected the two truly are. We could use a little reminding of these today. Christ purchased humanity in the fullness of his being: body, soul and spirit.

Christ did not save our spirit absent from our body. This might be best understood by examining humanity's state before the fall. When God created Adam and Eve, He created them perfect. His warning that to eat of the Tree of the Knowledge of Good and Evil, if disobeyed, would result in absolute death went unheeded, and thus, led to Adam and Eve's demise, both physically and spiritually. Though physical death was not immediate, spiritual death was instant. But thank God, before He created the very foundation of the world, He had already devised a plan. The fruition of such manifested in the person of Jesus Christ whose death, burial, resurrection and ascension saved and reunited us spiritually with God; our eternal destiny was forever sealed for all who would believe. However, was it only our spirit Christ saved? Of course, not, Christ saved both our spirit and body! *Do you not know that your bodies are temples of the Holy Spirit, who is in you, whom you have received from God? You are not your own; you were bought at a price. Therefore honor God with your bodies* (1 Corinthians 6:19-20a).

As members of Christ's body, what we do with our bodies, we essentially do with Christ. You can view it this way. When I get in my car and go to the store, my spirit does not depart from my body. My body and spirit are one; they go together. Likewise, since I am one with Christ in both body and spirit, wherever I go, Christ goes with me. The oneness we now have with Christ, therefore, should determine how we conduct our entire being inclusive of our bodies (see Romans 12:1 for further confirmation). Since everything we do is in light of Christ, this comprises our sexual behavior as well.

God has given us His instruction on everything from how we think, love, behave, work, speak, and even eat. Why would we then think that sex would be off limits, particularly, since it is the most intimate act we engage in with another human being? I know it may come as a surprise to many, but, yes, Christ is concerned about our sexual attitude and behavior too!

This supports Paul's rhetorical question in verse 15. *Do you not know that your bodies are members of Christ himself? Shall I then take the members of Christ and unite them with a prostitute? Never!* His question harks back to the Old Testament texts, when the Israelites would often commit sexual immorality by fornicating with foreigners and worshiping their foreign gods, a serious and punishable offense. In fact, God considered it idolatry or prostitution against Him whenever the Israelites committed such acts (see Numbers chapter 25 as an example). Paul's point is to make the analogy that just as God disdained the act of the Israelites prostituting themselves with foreign gods, a believer having sex with an unbeliever is, in God's eyes, an act of prostitution.

For Paul to define sex between a believer and unbeliever as an act of prostitution is for him to essentially perceive it as an offense against God. The believer, having God's Spirit dwelling within, has fornicated with one outside of Christ. Paul, wanting to elucidate further God's view of the physicality of the act and the spiritual union between Him and a believer, does two things in verses 16b and 17.

First, by referencing Genesis 2:24 in verse 16b, he juxtaposes the sexual oneness created between converted Corinthians and a prostitute and that shared between a husband and a wife. His purpose is to evince that two bodies joined together, sexually, become one whether between two Christians or not. Secondly, Paul, recognizing the deeper spiritual meaning, employs the conjunctive sentence in verse 17. For the Christian, everything that we do is in light of Christ. Thus, Paul reminds the Corinthians of their spiritual union with God, a union that is eternal because of the blood-bought redemption of their souls. In light of this union, since the believer has God's indwelling Spirit, sexual intimacy between a believer and an unbeliever becomes sexual idolatry. It's tantamount to the Israelites prostituting with foreign gods. Therefore, as you can see, God will get up in our sexual business! Our sex life does matter!

Just before I leave this matter, there is one more thing necessary to discuss. Reflecting upon Paul's teaching in verse 16, does this mean that it's permissible for two unmarried believers to engage sexually?

Well, one could infer that but for one caveat. Paul expressly states in verse 18a, *Flee sexual immorality,* (New King James Version). The Greek word for sexual immorality is *porneia,* which includes within its definition adultery; prostitution of one's self, idol worship as well as the act of fornication (sex between two unmarried people). It's interesting to note that the New Testament references sexual immorality (fornication) or sex outside of marriage 22 times in the New Testament of the King James Version and it's usually in the imperative.

So what does this all mean for single Christians? Simply this, if two unmarried believers are having sex then that, too, is to commit sexual immorality. The fact that they are Christians or believers is irrelevant. What constitutes sexual immorality, in this case, is the fact that they are unmarried.

*The legality of sex is found in God's Word.* Deemed imperative enough to entreat three times, the Beloved's warning caused me to ask, why does sex and marriage seem as two mutually inseparable bonds, and what about them is so important that she found it necessary to implore us to refrain if one was absent from the other? More importantly, why would the Word of God tell us to abstain from sex until marriage?

Honestly, she was not the reason I raised such questions. I have asked them of myself for years and many have asked me directly for my perspective. Now, I am even asked by the younger generation and that makes me happy. They want and deserve to know a biblical answer and not just someone's opinion, especially since we live in a world where information is plentiful and accessible in a myriad of ways in seconds. Their questions are logical and teaching is necessary.

What about those of us, who are older, born, reared and well acquainted with church and the Bible? Perhaps the church does not broach the subject as much as it needs to, so people are making uninformed choices or choices rendered from other sources that do not align with Scripture. Since there are so many questions about when and with whom, why not consult *the Source*. For Christians, the Word of God should always be our starting point for answers. It is the Word by which we are to live, not personal opinions.

For instance, many seem to embrace more readily the views of celebrity Christians and those outside the faith rather than the Word of God. Point in case, a question I hear people raise quite often concerns the so-called "90-day rule", which is the length of time one should wait before having sex with the person to whom they are dating and unmarried. The question used to be, "Is fornication wrong," or "Is that in the Bible?" Now, the question is how long one dates before having sex! Questions are being raised, just not the right ones. Rather than questions about the 90-day rule, I think there's another question we should raise first. How about, "In God's eyes, when is sex acceptable between two people?"

Well, I know I'm probably going to give some news many would rather not hear, but here it is. There is no biblical basis for the "90-day rule". I'm sorry, but not all advice is good or correct. What we need is a good dose of truth, and hopefully, that is truly what we are seeking. If our aim is to attain biblical truth, it first needs to be stacked up against God's Word for alignment, and if it fails then discard it. To do otherwise, would be tantamount to the blind leading the blind.

Let me say from the outset, I am not prudish. I acknowledge that sex is a beautiful thing; God created it! Neither the Church nor I am being asked to espouse a message that sex is off limits, bad or sinful. It is quite the contrary! The answer as to the proper time for sex is right in Scripture, without a doubt. Since the beginning of creation, marriage and sex went together. The two are mutually inseparable because they were God's design and intention right from the very beginning in the Garden of Eden.

*The presentation.* God presents Eve to Adam and Adam responds, *This is now bone of my bones and flesh of my flesh; she shall be called 'woman' for she was taken out of man* (Genesis 2:23). Verse 24 states that it is the reason, *a man leaves his mother and father and is "united" to his wife, and the two become one flesh.* This is all during the presentation of Eve to Adam.

The term for woman *and* wife is the same Hebrew word, *'ishshah.* Therefore, verse 24 could have read this way, "…is united to his woman." Instead, God chose to use the word wife. Why use a different word? There is a simple answer for this – both the word woman and wife are interchangeable for they have the same meaning. May I vehemently suggest to you that God in all of His wisdom purposely uses the word wife to make His purpose in creating man and woman unequivocally lucid? God's creation of Eve fulfilled more than Adam's need for a confidant and friend. She was so much more than one to share his landscaping plan for the east side of the Garden of Eden or to explain why he named the animals as he did. No, God satisfied His own recognition of that which He deemed "not good" (man's aloneness), with the creation and presentation of Eve to Adam, specifically, as his wife.

God's determination in the suitability of Adam's helpmeet and the intentionality that he not be alone was intrinsic in the creation of marriage. In other words, God's response to both Adam's aloneness and the suitability of his mate was answered by the creation of marriage. Marriage is the concept, but the tangibility of the concept was manifested with the joining (or perhaps more apt, the disjoining) of the first two people on earth. Hence, Eve came forth from Adam's side, not his back, or his foot. Do you see where I am going? God was intentional in the nature of Eve's formation. For Eve to actually come forth from Adam's own person is as close as a couple can get; thus, as a concrete demonstration of God's concept of marriage, God purposefully removed an integral part of Adam's anatomy to create Eve.

What do I mean? Well, perhaps it may seem extreme to say that Eve was already within Adam and it only took the removal of one of his ribs for God to create another one of His masterpieces. Perhaps this was God's ideal divine design for marriage. That two people be so close that they seemingly were knit together from the same body.

Interestingly, God used Adam's rib to form Eve. Although God only took one rib, consider the overall functionality of the rib cage; it is designed to protect some pretty vital organs such as the heart, the organ not only essential to life, but the seat of love and the center of emotions. It also shields our lungs, which regulates our air supply, but it also represents, metaphorically, the breath we sometimes lose when we are in love. Even more fascinating, the rib cage is flexible and can expand and contract by the action of the muscles of respiration.

What an ingenious way of evincing that as two lovers become one, they should be adaptable and flexible with one another as they mature. These lovers recognize that they were brought together to support one another and they also understand the importance of flexibility, able to give and take. Great relationships are sustained because there is an understanding between the two that disagreements must be handled amicably. Each person must learn to give up his or her need to be right and to be humble and submissive, in order to have a healthy and mature relationship. That in marriage, it's necessary to allow each other space to breathe maintaining their sense of identity, but never to the point that their separateness impedes their oneness. They also recognize that they need each other to be fully able to stretch, develop into, and experience all that God desires for their lives.

As suggested, if Eve was already inside of Adam, close enough to hear his heart beat, it might explain why at first sight Adam uttered the words concerning her, *bone of my bones and flesh of my flesh* after having discerned the spiritual connection and bond created between them. Eve was not his girlfriend, friend with benefits or live-in companion but rather he understood the much richer and deeper purpose of God. Eve was his wife.

For that reason, a man is to leave his family and begin a new life with his wife and that only after making the commitment to leave and unite as one are they then permitted to become one sexually. The term unite means to be glued or stuck together, to become inseparable as if one body! Having already been addressed, we know that sexual intercourse is two becoming one and now we know that the marital union is to occur first. God is a God of order.

Notice that they did not begin their relationship as boyfriend and girlfriend, but husband and wife. Yes, they did not have any others to choose from, but I wonder if that was a part of God's perfect plan as a message for us today. From the beginning, Adam understood that their relationship was not to be experimental, a test or trial run. If we know that we desire marriage, if we know that we want a life-long partner to share our lives, our dreams, visions and goals, then the decision to date anew is in order. Thus, we should seek God in prayer to reveal, order our steps, and position us to meet our mate.

The decision to have someone in your life takes a maturity level encompassing sincerity and integrity. This means that we do not sleep around or play around with other people's lives in any way until we discover "the one". I know some believe that the way to find the right person for them is to date multiple people simultaneously. I suppose this is not a problem if you are upfront and apprise everyone you are dating of what you are doing; they deserve to know so that they can make an informed decision as to whether or not they want that kind of relationship. Remember, we are Christians and should, *Do to others as you would have them do to you* (Luke 6:31).

Additionally, we must also understand that there are limitations in the manner we conduct ourselves in a relationship. Said another way, we are to treat those we date with the utmost respect, as a brother or a sister in the Lord, ...*but be thou an example of the believers, in word, in conversation, in charity, in spirit, in faith, in purity* (1 Timothy 4:12b).

So, my friends, it is marriage that makes sex legal. Hebrews 13:4 states, *Marriage should be honored by all, and the marriage bed kept pure, for God will judge the adulterer and all the sexually immoral.* The marriage bed, the place where married people are sexually intimate is the only bed that is undefiled. The emphasis is not about the place as much as it is about the condition under which sex is honored and the condition is marriage. Marriage makes sex holy and legal. In fact, just think. God doesn't prevent us from sexual expression and freedom. Quite the contrary, He simply provides the circumstance under which it is permissible and that is within the covenant of marriage. In marriage, couples can legally have all of the sex they desire!

# *Cool Fall*

W ell, as they say, "all good things must come to an end". Well, not exactly as in finished, over, done or fizzled out. Fall can mean those things, but it can also mean that the fire that used to send your heart racing with excitement at the sight of each other has slowed to a more moderate pace. You still like each other and want to be together, but some of the spark has begun to fizzle. This does not mean that you want to throw in the towel and give up. It's a normal state of affairs after the newness and excitement of anything has worn off. Albeit, it may be a sign of something graver if you have only been in relationship for a little while and already you are tired of each other. I will tackle that in a moment. For now, let us focus on the relationship that simply needs some sprucing up.

Fall happens in many relationships. When it does, you want to pray for understanding as to what it means for yours.

Fall is a time when things begin shifting or falling away. After summer has gone, verdant trees begin to lose their leaves, many of summer's flowers have died, and the glorious sights and exuberant sounds of our surroundings have slowly ebbed away indicating that fall has arrived. Green leaves morph into golds, yellows and reds, mums are planted and pumpkins adorn steps and gardens. Fall is a beautiful season even if summer has passed.

Though our surroundings look different, our address remains the same. I would not change my address simply because my gardenias, hydrangeas, or birds of paradise are no longer in bloom, leaves are crinkled beneath my feet, or I no longer hear as many birds singing perched in the trees. We do not move to a warmer climate in order to maintain our environment; my surroundings may have changed, but I can still do something so that it's just as pretty and appealing. Through use of our creativity, we must seek ways to enhance where we live so that the beauty to which we are accustomed and desirous of remains. So, how do we enhance our environment, or in our case, what can we do to bring life back into a relationship that seemingly is falling away?

*Spruce it up!* What many couples fail to do is to keep things fresh and alive. In our natural gardens, we replace the hydrangeas with mums and rake the leaves multiple times. We don't leave our garden unattended for eventually it will look ugly as if no one lives at our house and that is not what any of us wants. Relationships like gardens take work and lots of it! In fact, I assert that after God, the marriage relationship should be that which we devote most of our time.

Remember, God made us in His image and part of His image is His creativity. We should always want to learn and explore because we are forever evolving. I believe many couples err because they stop growing. This may be more prevalent between married couples, but unmarried people can fall into this rut too, particularly with time. It's not necessarily a compatibility issue; it's simply that people fail to nurture their relationship. It will be a great benefit if unmarried couples learn this prior to marriage.

One of the things I love most is talking to people and finding out their stories. I also love encouraging people and inspiring them to understand their usefulness to God's Kingdom. I am not nosy; there is a difference. I am genuinely interested in people. I love to talk to people, particularly those who rose above adverse circumstances and made it. Their perseverance won out. The mere fact that they persevered tells me that they employed work.

A cool fall does not necessarily mean that your relationship has gone south (technically, it would seem it got hot, right? I digress). You are settling in your relationship, but the newness and vitality is wearing off. It does not mean you do not love each other anymore. You simply need to understand what it will take to bring your relationship to another level and commit to just that.

I read in a few places, that on average, this happens to newlyweds between about the third to fifth year. Couples must abandon their inhibitions, think outside of the box, and always remain a student of each other. Since we are constantly evolving, we should continuously desire to grow in exploration of God's gift to us – the gift of each other. A healthy relationship cannot afford laziness. The older we become the more there is to know and learn about one another because we have experienced life that much more.

*Till your garden.* Any good gardener who wants to keep their garden looking good regardless of the season works at it. I cannot stress it enough. If you want a good relationship, you must work to get and keep it. If you deem your mate to be worth the keep, then you must do the work. We cannot just expect things to happen; some things call for us to be intentional. Constantly talk to each other, find out the goals, dreams and aspirations of your mate for they do change with time. Discover each other's likes, dislikes, and if you in some way are doing something that triggers negativity in that regard, work to change that.

As a part of getting to know one another better, learn more about your personality differences. This does not necessarily mean that you are incompatible; you must simply learn what each other's strengths and weaknesses are and how to make them work for you as a couple.

*Be considerate.* Remember special days like birthdays and anniversaries. You may have to write them down or put them on the calendar in your phone so as not to forget. Be conscious of the little things your mate tells you. Plan ahead even if it means getting a little help from others. Read books and articles that aid you in this area. There are lots of resources. You just have to do your homework.

*Beware of the enemy.* Be quick to apologize and make room on your calendar to discuss things that upset you so that you do not give the enemy an opportunity to exploit things. Also, be careful of outsiders with whom you discuss your relationship. What I mean by that is not everyone needs to know your business. Though it's sad to say, not everyone who smiles in your face is truly happy for you, even among Christians. There are still busybodies in churches and in some of our families who seek to stir up mess. This is something that you both must agree upon and adhere.

*Seek help, if necessary.* Not every spat calls to dissolve the relationship. Sometimes, a relationship could benefit from outside counsel. If your church has a Christian relationship counselor, it might behoove you to talk with them. And as I've already mentioned, read books on relationships. There are plenty written on various topics to help you resolve your particular relationship issues.

As a couple, perhaps the two of you will find as your relationship progresses, that you truly are incompatible and it may be time for you to move on. This is a perfect segue to my next point.

*After raking the leaves, it's time to get rid of them.* Where I lived as a child, our garden was raked and then the leaves placed at the curb. Later, they were picked up by the town's facility crew and hauled away. The raked garden was not finished nor did it truly look pretty until the entire process was complete, which included the pick up of the leaves.

The fall season of relationships can be almost as bad as the winter season because it's a time when your relationship may experience falling, raking and then being taken. In other words, it may come to an end. Not everything is meant to be and only the honest will be able to accept this fact. Perspective is crucial, for as I have said, there is always something beautiful to see in every season.

Breaking up does not have to leave one heartbroken because some breakups are worth it. If we are praying through the course of the relationship, then should it end, we can walk away with minimal to no regrets and heart damage because we will know that it's within the will of God. He is protecting us and, certainly, if marriage is in our future, God has someone else for us.

In his sermon, "The Will of God", T. D. Jakes states, "God's will is not to make us feel good. God's will is to woo us into the place He needs us to be." Is that not our ultimate goal, to be where God predestined us to be and have what God wants us to have?

My encouragement to you is to pray for a proper perspective. As long as I have waited to be in a fulfilling, loving relationship, what I've wanted and have waited for is the man that God decided I'd walk along side a long time ago. Admittedly, it has taken longer than I anticipated or wanted, but I can look back over my life and thank God for keeping me through every season, teaching me lessons along the way. Perhaps what I appreciate most is that I adhered to those lessons. I know I am blessed even more because of it.

My prayer and hope for you is that you too will allow God to lead and guide you through each season. Your mate is on the way. Keep trusting and praying. Never give up.

# *My Prayer for You*

*H*eavenly Father, I lift each person who has read this book to You. I pray that they experience an even deeper relationship with You and that You will lead, guide and protect them through each season. Bless them with the strength they need not to be anxious, or involved with anyone that You have not called to their lives. Bless them with wisdom and discipline as they engage in the relationship You have for them. Grant them the ability to abstain from everything until its proper time and at the proper time, bless them with the beauty of marriage according to Your Word. May they have the patience to always continue learning, never tiring of exploring and understanding their mate. Let them walk in a spirit of love and integrity, respect and honor, always esteeming the other higher than themselves.

We bless You now and believe that it is done according to Your divine will. Amen.